Fast Faces

Unleash Your Creativity with a Friendly Lump of Clay

JONNi GOOD

Wet Cat Books, Hendricks, MN

More books by Jonni Good, with inspiring ideas and creative projects that make sculpting fun and affordable:

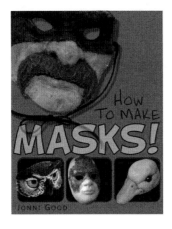
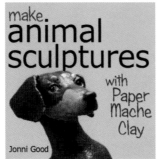

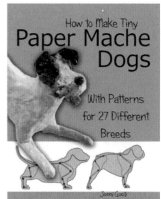

_____

Fast Faces: Unleash Your Creativity With a Friendly Lump of Clay
ISBN 978-1-7321063-0-7

Wet Cat Books
400 Cottage Ave.
Hendricks, MN 56136

WetCatBooks.com

This book was written for people of
all ages who know, as children do,
that we need to make stuff.

ART — iT'S MEDICINE FOR THE SOUL.

A QUICK NOTE TO KIDS:

Most books about art are written either for kids *or* adults, but not this book. (I've never been very good about following the rules.) If you like messing around with clay and you can read the instructions in the book, you'll have fun making Fast Faces. It doesn't matter how old you are.

This book will show you how to sculpt clay faces in a new way that makes every single one of them totally unique. They're definitely *weird*, too, but that's part of the fun.

Practicing the Fast Face method will also help you see details most people miss, and that's an important skill no matter what kind of art you make or what subjects you choose to draw or sculpt. Your art teacher will approve of that.

And besides, this book gives you a good excuse to get some silky wet clay on your hands (it feels really good), and to make goofy characters you might want to use as models for your animated videos or your next graphic novel.

I added a few notes about subjects that just happen to interest me, like the fact that many people use the word 'talent' all wrong, and why making art — even silly art like these Fast Faces — can make someone happy. I put those notes inside colored boxes so you can easily skip them if you think they're boring. I won't mind.

Have fun!

A QUICK NOTE TO GROWN-UPS:

The clay faces you'll see in this book were sculpted quickly and spontaneously, but they're not just for kids. We *all* need a little goofiness in our lives, no matter how old we are. Sometimes we also need a stress-free excuse to make something just for ourselves — and if we giggle while we work, that's even better.

Although these faces are fast and easy to create, even for beginners, they teach some very important skills that will benefit professional artists, too — like how to see details we don't usually notice, and how to find inspiration everywhere we look. They also remind us to be delighted by happy accidents, and that art is supposed to be fun.

I've been sculpting with many different media for many years, but I learn something with every new Fast Face I make — and every one of them surprises me. Why should kids have all the fun?

Enjoy!

CONTENTS

1. Getting Started

2. Fast Faces

3. Other Stuff

INTRODUCTION

This book is very different from anything I've written before. I'm known for teaching simple, easy methods for creating realistic sculptures. This book is the opposite — it's about creating intentionally *unrealistic* sculptures that turn out in excitingly unexpected ways.

I discovered the Fast Face method by accident. I'd been working for three days on a clay portrait based on several photos I found online. It wasn't going well. The eyes weren't right and the forehead wasn't wide enough. I'm sure you've had projects that go like that, too.

I almost gave up on it because I wasn't having any fun, but I decided to go ahead and fix that forehead with a little more clay, just to see if it would help.

I pulled a lump of clay out of the bag and I was about to pull off a small piece of it when I glanced down at the clay in my hand — and someone was looking back at me. There was a face already on that new lump of clay, *and I didn't put it there.*

Or, I should say there was a *suggestion* of a face. The mouth was there, below an unreasonably large muzzle area (for a human, anyway). It had a big bump for a nose, but it was way too high, and there were two scratches and dips

where the eyes would go. It didn't have much of a chin, and it had no forehead at all, but it didn't seem to matter. I liked the little fellow.

I put the 'real' portrait to the side and started to work on the little fist-sized lump. I tried to stay faithful to the suggestions on the clay, but I used my tools and fingers to define the features a little more clearly.

Then I gave him an ear and a collar, and two fuzzy old-man eyebrows. The face was done in just a few minutes. As you can see in the photo above, even after I worked on it with my sculpting tools there was still nothing *right* about that little face. In fact, it was all wrong — but it had more life in it, and more personality, than the portrait I'd been fussing with for days. And it was definitely more fun to make.

I named him Oscar, and I liked him so much that I made a plaster cast so I could keep him.

While I worked on Oscar it didn't feel like I was *working* at all — I was playing. I was discovering. I was exploring. I was *totally* focused, the way you get when you're in the middle of an exciting game and you're still not sure if you'll win or lose. But it was a nice short game that took only took a few minutes of my time.

I was hooked, and I had to tell people about this delightful new way to create surprising new characters in clay.

What's so great about Fast Faces?

If you spend a few minutes every day making silly faces based on the random marks you find in a lump of clay, the following things may begin to happen:

- **You'll gain confidence** in your ability to create truly original works of art. From the very beginning, every piece you make will be entirely unique.
- **You'll learn something new** with every new Fast Face you sculpt. You can then use that knowledge in other forms of art — like drawing and painting — and even for your next 'serious' sculpture.
- **You'll start to see details** all around you that you didn't notice before. The human mind isn't built to notice details, so this is something all artists need to learn how to do.
- **You'll have so many ideas** for new pieces that you can't possibly use them all. Inspira-

tion will be all around you, just waiting for you to notice.
- **You'll learn to embrace happy accidents** — and you'll also discover that not-so-happy accidents are no big deal. There's no 'right' way to create these faces. That means there's no 'wrong' way to do it, either.
- **Your own creative voice** will begin to take center stage as you notice common themes and styles spontaneously developing in your work.
- **You'll have a new craft** to teach to your friends. Why not throw a Fast Face party? Anyone from Middle School age to retirees will giggle as they see the surprising new faces they made themselves.
- **If you stay mindful** of the process, you may experience a deep sense of focus and curiosity while you play with your clay, and you'll probably notice that it makes you feel good. You might even be a little happier for the rest of the day. Why should art therapists be the only ones who know how to harness the healing properties of art?

Practicing inspiration.

The faces in this book look silly (and sometimes weird), but there's one skill they teach that isn't silly at all. You'll be learning how to actively find inspiration instead of just waiting for it to happen.

Writers are notorious for experiencing debilitating fear when they look at a blank page. Painters sometimes feel that way when looking at an empty canvas, and many sculptors dread an unopened bag of clay. Why? Because this thought takes over: *Will the Muse speak to me today?*

If inspiration remains silent for too long, some people give up on art completely, and that's a real shame.

Fortunately for us, it *is* possible to learn how to find inspiration when we need it, instead of waiting for the mood to strike. In fact, as you practice your Fast Faces you'll be following in the footsteps of the great Leonardo da Vinci. He wrote this passage in one of his many notebooks:

"If you look at any walls spotted with various stains or with a mixture of different kinds of stones ... you will be able to see in it a resemblance to various different landscapes ... You will also be able to see divers combats and figures in quick movement, and strange expressions of faces, and outlandish costumes, and an infinite number of things which you can then reduce into separate and well conceived forms."

Yes, Leonardo could see an army in combat on a stucco wall, if that's what he needed for his latest commission. He was doing something that we all do naturally when we see a lion in the clouds or a face on the moon. Leonardo understood the value of this natural human ability, and he took the trouble to master it.

Leonardo was using a trick of the human mind that scientists call *pareidolia*: The tendency to perceive specific, often meaningful images in random or ambiguous visual patterns.* (Merriam-Webster)

You'll be using that mental trick when you search for faces in the random shapes and shadows on a ball of clay. The faces you make with the techniques in this book will teach your unconscious mind to find inspiration any time you need it — just like Leonardo did when he needed a new costume or a fighting soldier or a strange expression to spice up his latest painting.

I hope they'll also help you reconnect with your childish memories of how fun it is to play with wet clay. These faces are just for you — a fun way to learn how to discover inspiration whenever you need it, and to find your own creative voice.

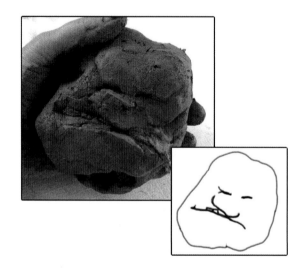

Do a Google Image search for the term pareidolia. You'll see some hilarious photos of knots in wood, mops, security cameras, onions and other everyday things that really do look like faces. It will make you giggle, I promise.

WHAT iS CREATiViTY?

I like the way Wikipedia defines creativity:

... a phenomenon whereby something new and somehow valuable is formed. The created item may be intangible (such as an idea, a scientific theory, a musical composition, or a joke) or a physical object (such as an invention, a literary work, or a painting).

We're all creative people. We may not be professional artists or architects or engineers, but we solve problems all day long. We learn things, we invent things, we build stuff, we find innovative ways to teach and do our jobs.

Creativity is an essential part of modern life. That's why there are so many books on the subject that are written for business people, mothers, teachers and others who need to find creative solutions to their daily problems.

How do we strengthen our imagination? As with any other skill, we get better at it with practice.

Larry Kim, founder and CTO of WordStream, wrote an article for Inc.com titled *9 Ways to Become More Creative in the Next 10 Minutes.*

Among other things, he suggested doodling; playing with toys; writing fast, short fiction (just for the fun of it); and signing up for a class to learn something new. Why would he suggest such playful ideas to 'serious' entrepreneurs and business-people? Because creativity happens spontaneously when we're having fun. The more we play, the more creative we become.

Fast Faces are fun. We sculpt them by finding patterns and relationships in random shapes on a ball of clay. Imagination is required, so every time we make a new Fast Face we're building our creative confidence.

That confidence might come in handy the next time we need to fix a broken pipe, or to market a new product, or to find a way to get along with an annoying coworker.

It can even help us create a new and unique piece of art.

Creativity is "giving the world something it didn't know it was missing." — Daniel Pink

TOOLS AND MATERIALS

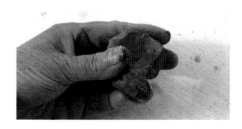

Wet Clay

WED Clay from the Laguna Clay Company (preferred) or wet clay from your local pottery supply store. The clay can be used many times, so one 25-pound or 12.5 kg bag is plenty. (See page 11.)

Fingers and Thumbs

Your hands are by far the most important tools when working with clay. (Your thumbs make great eye-sockets, for instance.) They also let you enjoy the silky-smooth texture of your WED clay. Don't worry — the clay washes off easily.

Sculpting Tools

You can use items you find in the kitchen, like the table knife shown here (I use it a lot!), or you can buy tools specially made for working with clay. (See page 12.)

Finishing Tools

If you want to smooth the surface of the clay after making your Fast Faces, you can use damp brushes in various sizes, or your fingers after dipping them in water.

And ...

A scrap of wood or a sculpting stand (optional) will hold your clay while you sculpt. (See page 13.) Paper towels and zip lock bags will keep your clay moist, and a plastic garbage bag placed on your table will keep it clean. And keep a damp paper towel handy to wipe off your hands in case the phone rings. Or better yet, you could ignore the phone or even (gasp!) turn it off while you work.

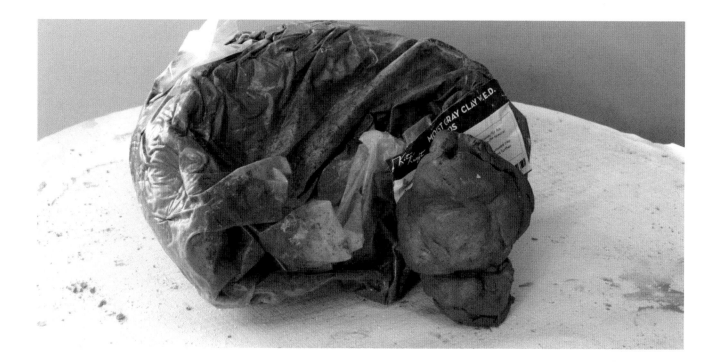

The Clay.

The Fast Faces in this book are all made with WED clay. This clay is wet, like pottery clay, but it has things added to it that make it better for sculpting. It was specially formulated for the animatronics designers at the Disney theme parks, and it's named after Walt E. Disney.

Many pottery supply stores and art supply stores in the United States carry WED clay, or you can order it from Amazon.com. (For a free downloadable materials list, see the Resources chapter at the end of this book).

If you're in the US and you have a store nearby that sells clay for potters, they might be able to order some for you. Tell them it's made by the Laguna Clay Company.

If you don't want to wait, or if you live outside the US where WED clay is not available at a reasonable price, ask the pottery supply store for a clay that's quite smooth, with very little grog (the gritty material that's added to pottery clay to help it hold its shape). Also tell them you'll be using it for small sculptures, but you won't be firing it.

Even though a regular wet clay will work for sculpting, (people have been sculpting with it for at least 35,000 years), I do recommend using WED clay if you can find some. It's specifically made for people who want to make sculptures quickly without sacrificing the ability to make fine details. That's why it's so great for sculpting our Fast Faces.

Unlike most oil-based modeling clays, WED clay doesn't need to be warmed up to make it usable because it's the perfect consistency right out of the bag. It's a *fast* clay because it's soft, but you can let it dry on the surface for a few minutes if you want a firmer clay for smaller details.

You can cover it with a plastic bag to keep it moist if you want to come back and work on it later, or you can just put the clay back in the bag and use it for another face tomorrow.

WED clay dries more slowly than regular pottery clay, and it tends to crack less as it dries. The gray color of the clay lets you see all the shadows cast by the forms, which makes sculpting easier, and it makes your finished pieces great models for drawing studies. The people who designed this product covered all the bases.

The downside of WED clay is that it's a *modeling clay*, and it can't be baked or fired in a kiln. In other words, it was not designed to be used as the final sculpture. However, if you create a

face that you fall in love with, there are quite a few ways to save it or share it with friends. I hid the chapter that explores those options in the back of this book, because I hope you'll use your Fast Face time for playful exploration instead of worrying about making a sculpture that's 'good enough' to save.

But, like I said — if this particular clay isn't available, don't let that stop you. A bag of wet clay from your local pottery supply store won't cost much and it will work just fine.

Sculpting tools.

The tools you use the most for these Fast Faces are your fingers and thumbs. However, you'll probably also want a few items that make it easier to model small details and to smooth the surface of the clay when the sculpture is finished.

I use a kitchen knife a lot, both to push the clay around and to cut off the back of a lump of clay so it will sit flat on my sculpting stand. If you don't have any other sculpting tools, you'll be surprised by the versatility of this tool you already have in your kitchen.

I prefer stainless steel wax carvers because they're small and perfect for fine details. You can sometimes find an entire 12-piece set for less than $8.

The sculpting stand.

You don't need to make a sculpting stand right away. Just put your clay on a scrap piece of wood, put it on a table or your lap, and start sculpting. You can even use a piece of cardboard that you cover with plastic tape or a clear plastic bag, although wood is better because the clay sticks to it when it's wet.

However, the stand makes it much easier to see your faces straight on so you're not always looking at the bottom of its chin and up its nose.

I made mine with a few pieces of scrap lumber. See instructions on the following page.

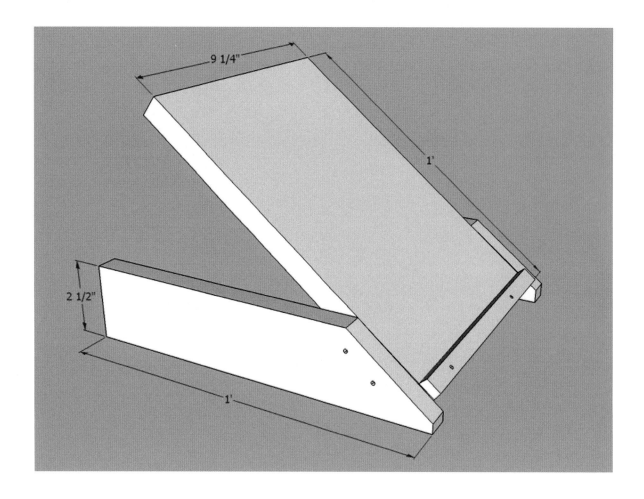

Materials for the sculpting stand:

- One (1) 12" piece from a scrap of 1" x 10" (19 x 235 mm) lumber.
- Two (2) 12" pieces of 1" x 3" or 1" x 4". (19 x 64 mm or 19 x 89 mm)
- Scrap of molding that fits the lower edge of your stand (optional).
- Four (4) 1.5" (3.8 cm) wood screws. Or use screws you have that are long enough.
- Two (2) small screws for the optional strip of molding.

Note: The actual dimensions aren't important. Just use what you can find as long as it's big enough to hold your Fast Face sculptures.

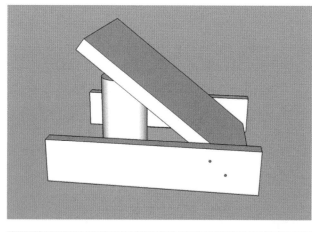

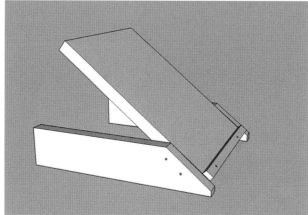

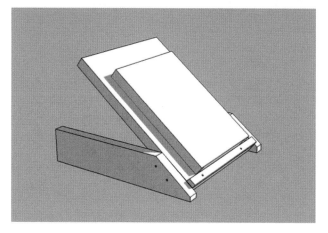

Assembly:

1. Put the pieces of wood on the table where you'll sculpt your faces. Prop up the large piece of wood with something that will keep it at the right angle. You want to be able to see your sculptures straight on. The wood will try to fall down, so a helper will make this project much easier.

2. Put the 1 x 3's on each side of the larger piece, as shown, and mark the spots for the screws. Drill pilot holes and then use two screws on each side to hold the 1 x 3's in place.

3. Cut off the front corners on the 1 x 3's to make your stand look nicer.

4. You can add an optional piece of scrap molding to the bottom of the stand. This lets you place your clay on a separate piece of wood and the molding keeps it from falling off the stand. This comes in handy if you want to work on more than one face at a time.

THE BASICS

Every face you make using the Fast Face method will start out differently, because the faces are based on 'suggestions' offered by random marks, bumps and creases in the clay.

Artists are unique, too, so everyone who makes a Fast Face will have a different goal in mind. You might want to spend a few minutes in an creatively-engaging task to reduce stress and recharge your batteries. If so, you'll do this very differently from a person who wants to create models for drawing studies, or someone who wants to discover his or her own creative voice. And people who have deprived themselves of all artistic activities in the past because of a mis-

taken belief that they're not 'talented' will approach these exercises differently, too.

For these reasons, in the following chapters I'll show you some of the faces I've made, and I'll write down some of the thoughts I had while I worked. Watch over my shoulder as I create the faces in this book. Then grab some clay and start making your own faces the way *you* want to do it.

As I mentioned in the Introduction, I follow just one rule (usually). I identify at least one face-like feature in the original ball of clay, and then I change that one feature *as little as possible* so I can still find it on the finished piece. You don't have to do it that way, but I hope you'll try it at least a few times because it's a lot of fun. It also proves that 'perfection' is not needed to create a believable sculpture.

I love it when I create a Fast Face that looks like someone I'd enjoy spending time with, or when it has a quirky personality that intrigues me. That doesn't happen every single time, but even the grumpy faces are fun to make. If you plan to learn something new every time you sit down and play with your clay, you *will* learn something, and that new knowledge may be as surprising as the face you just made.

As you continue to make your little faces, more and more inspiring shapes will start to appear when you take a new lump of clay out of the bag. In fact, when you have faces on your mind you'll probably start seeing them everywhere — on randomly patterned tiles, in the shadows on a tufted rug, and even on plastered walls, like Leonardo did.

It sounds weird, I know, but Leonardo's friends probably thought his wall-gazing trick was a bit weird, too — but that didn't stop him from using it to create great art.

Keep a record.

I highly recommend keeping a photo journal of your faces, with at least a snapshot of the *before* and *after* versions of each one — even the ones you don't like very much. That way, you'll be able to see how they change over time. Are they getting more playful? More realistic? Can you see your own individuality showing up in each new face you make? Do you like the way some of them worked, but not others? If so, is it because of the mood the faces express, or just because there are things you now wish you'd done differently?

If I had to give just one piece of advice:

Don't hurry! Take your time, relax, and have some fun.

How to take care of your clay.

Your clay will be in the perfect condition for sculpting when you open the bag, and it can only stay that way if you remember to keep the bag tightly closed. Once the clay in the bag dries out it can be a real challenge to get it back the way you want it.

I twist the top of the bag tightly, as shown below, and then turn it upside down. The weight of the clay keeps the twist from coming apart. If you forget to close the bag and the surface starts to dry out, put a damp paper towel inside the bag before closing it. Remove the paper towel after the clay has rehydrated.

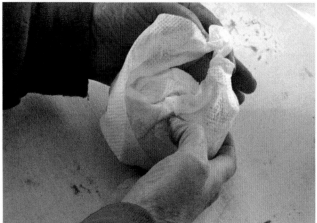

While you're working on a face.

When you need to take a break but you aren't finished working on a face, cover it with a plastic bag or plastic kitchen wrap. This will keep it damp overnight. If you need to leave it for more than a day or two, check it occasionally. If it starts to dry, put a damp paper towel under the plastic.

To make the clay usable for your next project.

When you're finished with a face, be sure to take care of the clay so you can use it again for another project. Check to see if it's still as soft as it was when you first took it out of the bag. If not, cover it with several layers of damp paper towel and stick it in a zip-top plastic bag. Leave it there for a day or two until it's soft again.

If the clay dried out completely when you made your face, it could take as long as a week to get soft again, and you might need to add more water to the paper towel after a day or two. You can feel how soft the clay is by squeezing the bag.

When it's time to use the clay for a new face, some parts might be soft while other parts are still stiff. Squish, fold and knead it to even out the moisture level, but do this *slowly*, because interesting new features might show up and you won't want to miss them.

Finding features in the clay.

Most people don't actively look for facial features in random shapes, although it often happens when you don't expect it. Doing it on purpose usually takes some practice.

You'll probably need to squish and manipulate your clay after you pull some out of the bag, because a perfectly smooth ball of clay doesn't have any face-like features to work with. Even though I like to say I'm letting the clay do much of the work, I have to encourage it to cooperate with me. As you read through the following chapters, I'll show you how I work with the clay until some features show up.

And remember — if your lump of clay has features that don't appeal to you, just squish it around a bit until you find something you like better. The clay is *helping*, but it's not in charge.

Don't get frustrated if your clay doesn't have any obvious features on it. As I mentioned in the introduction, it takes time and practice to find a face in a randomly shaped blob of clay. If you don't see anything at all, you can fold your clay like I did with my Cheerful Ogre (page 46) to make a mouth. That will be enough to get your started. Then, as you make more and more faces, it will get easier to find faces in the clay.

Take a look at the lumps of clay on this page. Then look at the drawings I made of the main features I decided to work with. If you had the same pieces of clay in your hand, you might find features on the other side that interest you more. You might see the same features I did, but decide to use them in a different way. Or you might decide to turn the ball of clay upside down, which would give you something entirely different to play with. There are always differ-

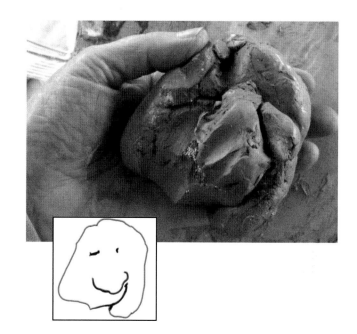

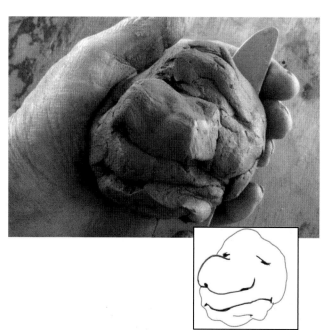

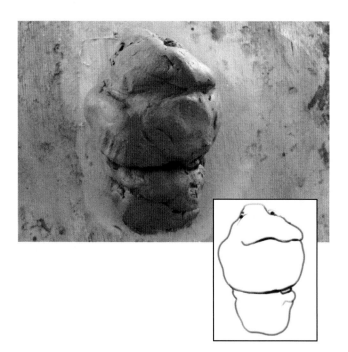

ent choices you can make, and different moods and expressions to explore.

If you have to squish and fold your lump of clay to make it show you a feature to start with, go slowly — if you hurry you could lose some features that would be a lot of fun to play with. When I go back and look at my *before* pictures, I often see features that I totally missed when the clay was in my hand. We need to slow down and pay attention to the clay.

Also remember that your lump of clay has more than one side — a great character might be hiding on the back.

When you identify a feature or an entire face in the clay, I recommend making a sketch of it, or draw over a photo of the lump in a graphics program, like I did. This helps you be more mindful of *all* the features on the lump of clay, and not just the first ones you notice.

Some lumps have more than one feature, or even the suggestion of an entire face, like the ones on the these pages. Sometimes you'll find features on two different sides. And if the only feature that shows up is a mouth, it's possible that the face you make could be either frowning or smiling, depending on which way you hold the clay.

As you're looking at the lumps of clay on this page, try to imagine how you would change them to make them into complete, finished sculptures. Your Fast Faces would probably come out very differently than mine did.

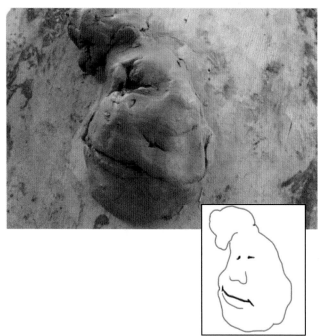

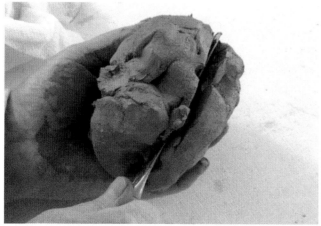

Preparing the clay for sculpting.

After you identify features that you want to work with, you need to press your clay onto a board or sculpting stand, as shown in the photos on this page. This is much easier than holding the clay in your hand while you sculpt. You can place the clay on the board so the face is looking straight at you, or put it at an angle so it's looking off to the side.

Use a knife to cut through the back to create a flat surface.

Be careful to not squish the clay too much while you cut, or you could lose the features you like.

Press the flat area against the wood, and gently rock or twist it so the wet clay gets a tight grip on the board. You're now ready to sculpt.

Sculpting your Fast Faces.

In the following chapters I'll show you a few of the Fast Faces I've made. In the spirit of honesty, I'll even show you some of the faces that didn't come out as nice as I wanted them to. I learn something even from those not-so-great faces, and I enjoyed making them. That's one of the best things about any art project. If a drawing or sculpture doesn't come out quite right, it gives us an excuse to make another one — and the next one will be even better because of the lessons we learned along the way.

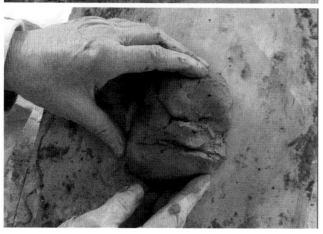

Finishing touches.

 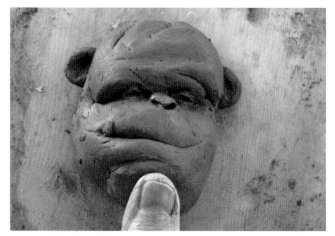

When you're finished sculpting, you may want your little face to have a smoother surface. You can use a damp brush to smooth the clay. A big brush works well on cheeks and chins, and a small artist's brush works well around the eyes and other smaller details. Don't get too carried away though, because it's easy to remove a small feature that doesn't seem important until it's gone.

To make the clay even smoother, you can run your thumb over the dampened clay. You can also give it a texture by pressing a bumpy paper towel into the damp clay, or by pouncing the ends of the brush bristles, gently, over the 'skin' to give it a rougher look. If you really like the face and want it to be more realistic, you can add wrinkles, and even a collar or scarf and a hat.

Then what?

If you fall in love with one of your faces, there are ways to save them or share them. I'll show you how in the Save and Share chapter at the back of the book.

TALENT, SCHMALENT

I often hear from people who avoided artistic activities for forty years or more because they were told, *way back when they were still in grade school,* that they weren't talented. When these folks finally decide to take up a creative hobby, their lives change in ways they never could have imagined. Quite often, their artistic skills are quite remarkable, in spite of their late start.

I think the *untalented* label is often applied in error because there's a lot of confusion about what talent *is*, and how important it may or may not be for future achievement in the arts. The meaning of the word is much more complicated than the simple dictionary definition would have us believe. Heck — even *scientists* don't know exactly what talent is.

Many people believe that talent makes it easy to create art, and that someone who struggles to learn an artistic skill *isn't* talented. That's not how it works in real life. If you ask a professional artist how she became so good at her craft, she'll tell you how many classes she took, how much money she spent on training, and how many hours she spent in her studio so she could gain the skill she needed to create a beautiful painting or sculpture. On the other hand, if you tell her how 'lucky' she is to be able to create such beautiful paintings so easily, you may get a reluctant smile and a sigh. She's probably a nice person, so her eyes will only roll when you're safely out of sight.

Many people also think talent can be identified when a child is still very young, but that's not always true, either. Some kids take longer to develop their fine motor skills and eye-hand coordination, so their early drawings may not show their full artistic potential. Many other people don't become interested in learning one of the creative arts until they're much older, perhaps not even until they retire.

I watched a video on Netflix about Chef Dan Barber. His brother said Dan showed no special talent when he was growing up. In fact, just before Dan was fired from his first job in a bakery, he overheard the owner saying "I've got to get that guy out of here before he puts me out of business." Yet Dan Barber has now received numerous top awards for his cooking and his achievements have been recognized by some of the most important people in the restaurant business. He made up for his lack of early talent by using his insatiable curiosity, his commitment to learning his craft, and his desire to produce exceptionally good food from natural ingredients.

Which proves that we can't predict *anyone's* future — not even our own.

So the question we should ask ourselves is not 'do I have talent?' but 'does this look like something I want to learn how to do?'

And that talent stuff? *Fuhgeddaboudit.*

GORILLA JIM

Before...

I wanted all of the faces for this book to be human (more or less), but you can never predict what (or who) will appear when you start squishing a ball of clay. As you'll see in later chapters, this was not the only non-human face that showed up.

I'm actually surprised that it didn't happen more often, because my house is filled with real and sculpted animals, and my shelves are sagging with books by wildlife photographers and about animal behavior and natural history. I would expect to see foxes or zebras or dogs in *every* lump of clay, but they usually look more or less like people.

Of course, if I gave this one a slightly bigger nose, he could have been a muscle-bound boxer who loses most of his fights, but this lump of clay said 'gorilla' to me.

Finding some features to work with.

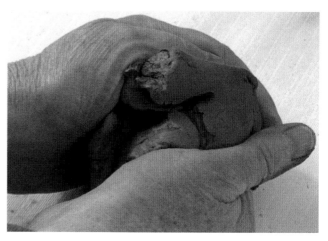

The first lump of clay you pull out of the bag might not have any recognizable features at all. Or maybe you see a feature or two but they aren't interesting enough.

If you can't find any features to work with, squish and pull the clay into a different shape.

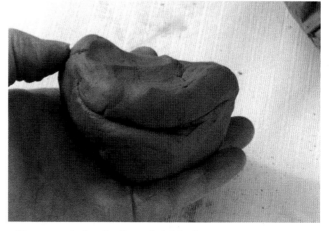

This came out the first time I squished my ball of clay. There *is* a nose and a mouth (can you see them?) but I wasn't inspired. I tried again.

I flattened the ball and folded it over. Now there's a mouth, but nothing else. This is actually a good start on a face, but it was very similar to one I'd already made.

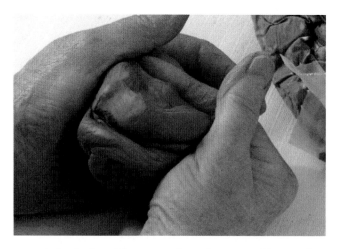

I squished the sides together, but it still wasn't doing anything interesting. I did a little more squishing, and then, in frustration, I pulled off a big chunk from the back and stuck it on top.

That's when I saw the beginnings of a gorilla in the clay. I liked the tiny nose bump, the shape of the mouth, the suggestion of a tooth and a very strong brow ridge. I was ready to sculpt.

Working with the features you find.

Once you have features to work with, you have decisions to make:

- Will you have the face looking straight at you while you work, or will you put it on the board so it's in profile or looking slightly to the side?
- Is there a specific feature that you'll leave entirely alone, or will you work with the general suggestions in the clay while giving them your own personal spin?
- And (this is an important question for me) what species are you sculpting? Animal? Human? Alien? Mythological?

Depending on your own particular goals, you might finish your face in a few minutes, leaving much of the original features as you found them — or you might be inspired by the original shapes you see on the clay but completely rework them into a finished piece over the course of an hour or more.

When you start your next face, there will be a whole new set of decisions to make, but over time you'll discover certain ways of sculpting that feel more comfortable to you. Your unique creative voice will assert itself and begin to show up in your work.

I used my table knife to slice some clay off the back to make it flat.

Next I pressed the clay firmly against the board. This can be tricky, because the clay is still soft. Handle it carefully but firmly, pressing it onto the board and then twisting it a little so it grabs on tight.

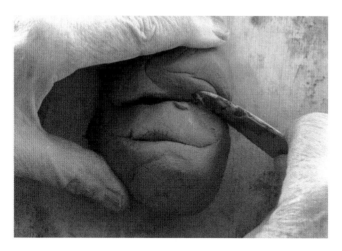

My gorilla had a brow but no space for eyes. I used my knife to push up on the clay to create eye sockets.

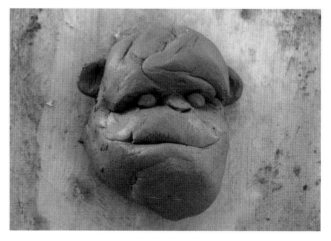

Tiny balls of clay were pressed into the new eye sockets. The nose was defined by pressing gorilla-like nostrils into the small nose-like bump between the eyes. And I added small ears, because I think he looks more like a gorilla than a big-eared chimp.

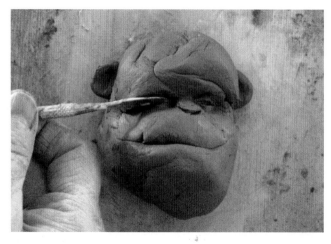

I flattened the eyes so there would be no deep empty spaces around them, and then quickly drew in open eyes with my wax carving tool. He became somewhat melancholy at that point — or maybe he's just ready for a nap.

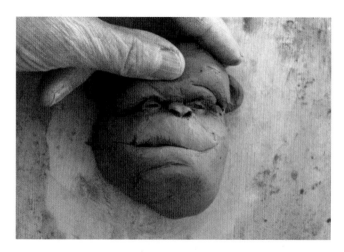

I deepened the line above his chin, just because I felt like it, and pushed into the clay above his eyes to make the brow ridge more gorilla-like.

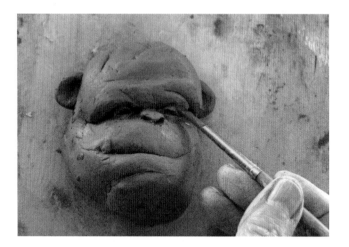

I opened the eyes a little more, and gave him a protruding tooth in the area where the upper lip was slightly broken. I smoothed the clay with a slightly damp brush.

After ...

What did I learn?

This is not a polished sculpture, and it doesn't really look like a gorilla, but I know my next portrait of a *real* gorilla will have more personality — and it will feel more playful — because I messed around with this small ball of clay.

I'm also starting to notice that my little faces often reflect my own moods. I like the idea of my sculptures representing who I am, and we're *all* slightly different from one day to the next. Why shouldn't our sculptures be different, too?

CAN ANYONE LEARN TO DRAW OR SCULPT?

Yes, it's true — and I can prove it. Can you write your own name? Yes? Then you can draw. Back in grade school, your teacher showed you some random lines and squiggles on the board at the front of the class and you copied what you saw on a piece of paper. She corrected you when you drew lines in the wrong place and cheered you on when you got it right. Then she made you do it again, and *again*, until those letters became part of your muscle memory. If you practice drawing the same way, it will eventually feel as natural as writing. And yes, you can learn to sculpt that way, too. Musicians practice. Athletes practice. Artists need to practice, too.

Before...

SMILING JACK

When I pulled this lump of clay out of the bag, I could definitely (almost) see the beginnings of a mouth, a nose and one eye. Part of the upper lip was also the lower border of the clay, so he has no chin at all. Weird, I know, but I found it very appealing.

When I go back and look at my *before* photos I always see different decisions I could have made. In this case, I wonder if I put one of his eyes is in the right place? And was that lower eyelid really necessary? Small details, I know, but there are always many choices. When you look at this silly lump of clay, what do *you* see?

How would you approach this session differently?

What did I learn?

I'm learning how important it is to keep looking for the features in the clay, both before and after I start moving it around. The clay offers unique suggestions that I never would have though of by myself. Create a face with no lower jaw, and call it good? I *never* would have done that before I started making Fast Faces. But I like this little guy.

Finding the features.

The crease on the lower right-hand side of the lump doesn't really look like a mouth — except that it does. In fact, it reminds me of those guys who talk out of the side of their mouth when they're telling a naughty joke. That gives Jack a personality I can work with before I make any changes at all.

There's already one almost-closed eye, and there's a shape that can be used for a nose. It will be a really *big* nose, though. Should I remove some of the clay to make the nose a more realistic size? I decided to follow the suggestion in the clay.

The extra lump of clay opposite the existing eye was a problem. What is it? I tried rounding it off to see if it would look like a monocle, and added a second eye above it so he could see out.

The monocle idea didn't work. You can see it not working in the top photo on the right.

No problem — I removed the blob. Then I added a second nostril to the nose. (The original nose bump already had one nostril.) There were several places where the new nostril could go, but the spot I chose seemed the most natural.

I added more clay to the nose to round it out and to remove the marks made by my fingers. Then I added just enough clay between the eyes to connect the nose to the forehead.

I added a hint of cheekbones on both sides, and the new eye got an upper eyelid and a bag underneath. If I hadn't tried the monocle idea, I probably would have made the second eye lower, but I'm OK with it where it is.

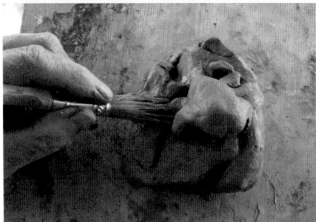

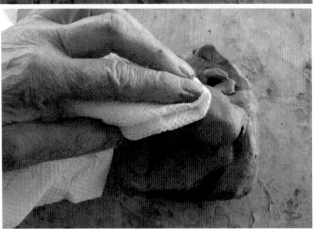

I gave him a stronger crease beside the muzzle. (That crease is called the nasolabial fold, or 'smile line,' in case you're wondering. Don't worry — it won't be on the test.) The crease helps balance the deep crease of the mouth and it made the face less flat. Besides, it just felt like it belonged there. I softened the cheek by running my thumb over it.

I added an eyebrow above the new eye, but left the suggestion of an eyebrow on the other side without changing it.

That's when I decided the sculpting was done.

To smooth the clay I used a damp brush and then a dry paper towel to smooth off the rougher parts of the sculpture. I let the surface dry for a few hours to firm up, and then I used the pads of my fingers to soften any brush marks that still remained.

When I look at the photos, I regret losing some of the rougher texture at the end of his nose. It added some character to the piece, but it's a minor issue and I'm not fretting about it.

When I came back to take one last photo, I decided it wasn't *quite* done yet. I added a few quick scratches to indicate hair on those eyebrows, and I gave him just a hint of a lower eyelid on one eye. I tried to do the same on the other eye, but I didn't like it. Decisions, decisions.

OK, *now* it's done, as you can see on the following page.

Other decisions I could have made.

The original shape that suggested a nose could have been reduced to make the proportions more realistic. Or the nostrils could have been placed lower down to give him a longer, thinner nose. Either change would have resulted in a completely different character.

He could have been female. In fact, I thought the original lump of clay looked like a girl with a pageboy haircut. I can't pinpoint the specific decision that changed the gender, but I think it happened when I tried out that monocle idea.

He could have been a different species. When I turned the original lump of clay in my hands, I saw the body and ears of a rabbit on one of the sides that I didn't show you. I turned it again and I saw the suggestion of a bulldog's chin. I chose the side I liked best, but it could have easily gone another way for a different, but very enjoyable sculpting session.

The expression on this piece changes when I turn him in my hands. One moment he's telling a joke, then he's sad, then he's squinting from spending too much time in the sun. His changeability would make him a good model for a bit player in an animated movie or an illustrated book for kids. Or maybe he could be the hero's faithful friend in a graphic novel. With a schnoz like that, he'd never be cast in the leading role.

After ...

SOURPUSS

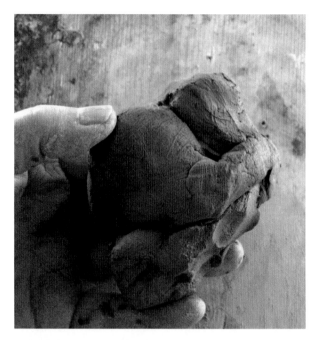

In this lump of clay (top photo) there's a good start on a nice Chinese Shar-Pei portrait (can you see it? The nose would be right below my thumb) but I was in the mood for a human face, instead. I kept squashing the clay, and the flat-nosed fellow shown at the bottom right finally appeared.

The clay now had a definite area for the eyes and a shallow forehead, a cheekbone on one side, and an oddly-shaped mouth. There's almost enough to give it a personality, but will I be able to stay faithful to the accidental face and still have it end up looking like something I did on purpose?

What did I learn?

The 'before' photo came in handy. During the sculpt I changed the look of this fellow, and then I changed it back again after seeing the original snapshot.
I'm discovering that even with the clay dictating some of the features, I'm starting to see more of my own personality coming through in my work. I'm also learning that I really enjoy designing strange characters. I never knew that before.

Before...

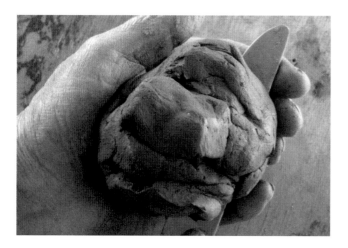

I used my table knife to cut through the clay.

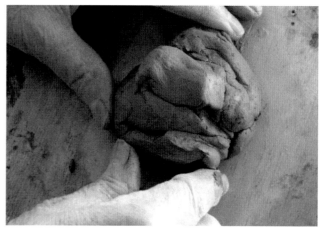

Then I pressed the flat back onto my sculpting board.

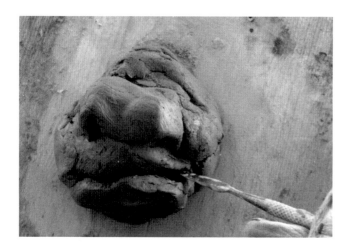

Part of the 'lips' were too strange, so I used one of my wax-carving tools to make them look more reasonable. During this part of the sculpt, he started to look like he was growling, and I wasn't quite happy with it.

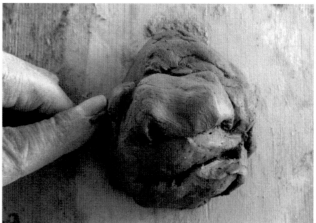

I added clay to give him another cheekbone.

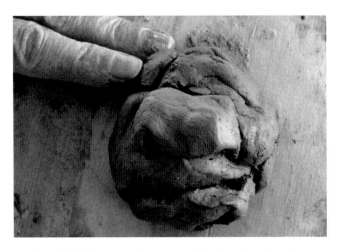

And I added more clay to make his forehead more symmetrical.

Using both thumbs at the same time, I pressed in some eye sockets above that weird flat nose.

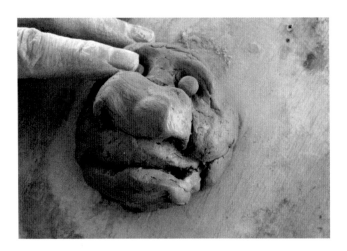

Small balls of clay were pressed into the eye sockets ...

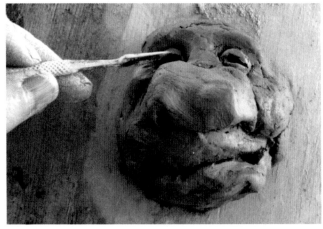

And I opened them up so he could see out. It's possible to get away with eyes like this when your face is small and goofy to start with. It probably wouldn't work on a fine portrait of your boss' wife.

The new cheekbone still needed more clay.

And I added a couple of eyebrows.

Almost done ...

Done ...

While I sculpted the mouth, I changed the lower lip, and I didn't like it. I looked at the snapshot of the original lump of clay, and then I used my thumb to push that lower lip so it was back the way it was before. He isn't such a Sourpuss any more, so maybe I should change his name, too.

Before...

FROGGY DUDE

I made many changes to this lump of clay when I created Froggy Dude - and then I changed most of it back to the way it started.

What did I learn?

When you're sculpting a realistic face and something seems just a bit off but you aren't sure why, there are several tricks you can use to figure it out. You can turn the sculpture upside down; you can look at it in a mirror; or you can get out your calipers to make sure you put the features where they belong.

But what if your face was never meant to be realistic, but it *still* doesn't feel quite right? In that case, the usual tricks won't work.

For this sculpture, I went back to the original photo of the raw lump of clay, the one you see above. With the photo as a model, I did a sculptural version of hitting the 'redo button.' Was it really an improvement? With a face as weird as this one, it's kind of hard to tell.

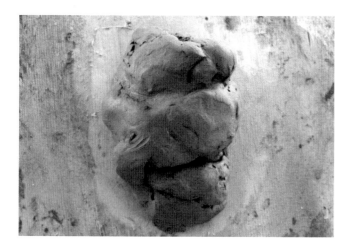

I added a button nose to the end of the sort-of nose-shaped area, and added a smile muscle beside the mouth.

Then I gave him an eye socket above the head, in a semi-froggy manner. Extra clay beside his nose was carved away, but enough was left to create a cheek just below the eye.

I added the eyes and used a brush to make the surface smoother.

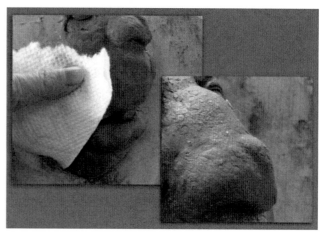

Then I pressed a bumpy paper towel onto the clay to give it a froggy skin texture.

This one?

At this point, I really thought it was finished. I left it sitting on the board for over a week because I wasn't excited about it. Of course, it completely dried out.

Then I went back and looked at the original photo at the beginning of this chapter. I decided to lose the froggy eyes and go back to the small eyes suggested by the clay. I also widened both his nose and his grin. To make the changes, I first softened the clay in a moist paper towel so the new clay would stick to it.

Is the latest version an improvement? I'm not sure. I like the new nose, but I miss the buck teeth and the big eyes. It was fun to play with it - but now it's time to move on and do something else.

Or this one?

HAVE YOU FOUND YOUR CREATIVE LANGUAGE?

There are thousands of creative languages. Your creative language could be baseball, or drawing, or training dogs. Someone else's special language could be gardening, molecular science, computer programming, weight lifting, sculpting, music, cooking or crossword puzzles. It's a craft or hobby that sparks your curiosity and interest, and you feel compelled to learn how to do it well.

You find your own special interest by trying as many different things as possible. Some people are practically born knowing what their special hobby or creative activity is, but other people keep looking for years.

The search itself can be rewarding.

Temple Grandin, the author of *Animals Make Us Human*, tells us that curiosity is one of the basic emotions in all animals (and in humans, too). As with the other basic emotions, like fear and anger, we're born with a natural capacity to be curious and to seek out answers to interesting puzzles.

According to Dr. Grandin, we feel really good when we're in a state of intense curiosity.* That may be one of the reasons why art projects are so much fun. When you sit down with a pencil and paper or a blob of clay you get to answer a dozen questions, like where do the eyes go, and how thick should I make this mark? Then, when all the decisions have been made, you get to start a *new* drawing or sculpture, and you answer those questions all over again. But this time, the answers will be different because you're creating something new.

You see, one of the things about curiosity is that you can't feel curious about something you already know. You can only feel the excitement of discovery when you're discovering something you've never discovered before.

This means that your special creative language or hobby needs to be just challenging enough so you always have something new to learn. If it's too easy, you'll get bored and go do something else. But it can't be too difficult to learn, either. If it's too hard, or if you need training that isn't available to you, you'll give up in frustration.

Once you find a project or hobby that keeps your curiosity firing at max capacity for at least a few minutes every single day, you'll have found your own special creative language. And it's quite possible that you'll be a happier person, too.

That's true for animals, too, and it explains why our pets need games, walks and challenging activities. They aren't truly happy unless they use their curiosity and intelligence every single day.

STYLIN' SAM

This lump of clay started out as two lumps that were used for other projects. When I was done playing with them I wrapped them in wet paper towels and put them in a zip-top plastic bag. When I pulled them back out of the bag to start this new Fast Face, one piece was drier and stiffer than the other piece, so I started to squish them together to even out the moisture levels.

After a few pushes and turns, I noticed the makings of an almost complete face. This begins to happen more often as you rework your clay. I don't know if there are more creases and bumps on each lump because we've already made faces with them, or if we've just had more practice seeing features in the random shapes.

This lump already has a mouth, a nice cheekbone on one side, and a prominent nasolabial fold.

With that big hole in the middle of his forehead, it could have been a Cyclops. I went for the more traditional human template, instead, and gave him two eyes.

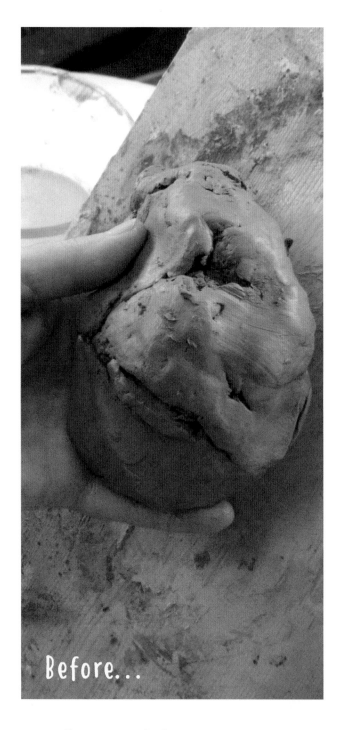

Before...

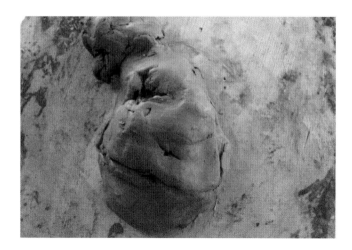

After it was flattened onto the board, I had to decide if I would keep the blob of clay at the top or remove it. I left it on to represent hair. It's strange, but I like it.

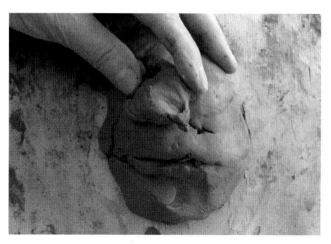

I pulled a small piece of clay from the bag and put it where the nose should go. It already has a suggestion of nostrils. It's also very crooked, but I liked that, too.

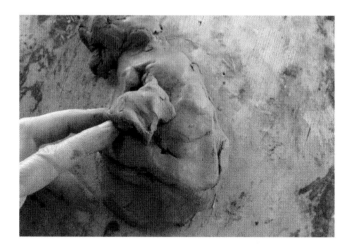

I stuck my finger up his nose to define the nostrils ...

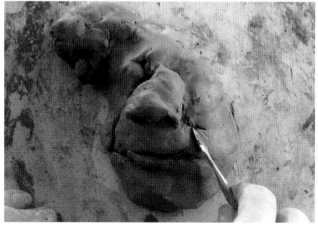

... and added another crease to match the one on the other side.

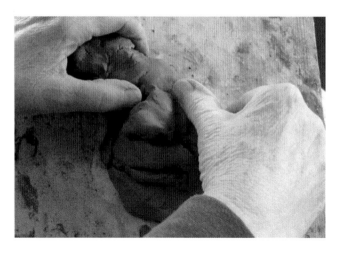

I pressed both thumbs into the clay beside the nose to make depressions for the eyes. It's easier to make them the same if you do them both at once.

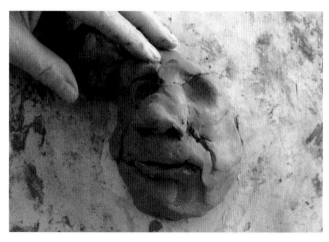

He needed more of a brow ridge above one eye.

And he needed an ear. I just pushed some of the clay from his cheek towards the board. It isn't realistic, but it works.

He already seemed to be smiling on one scorner of his mouth, so I added an exaggerated bit of muscle at the other end to match.

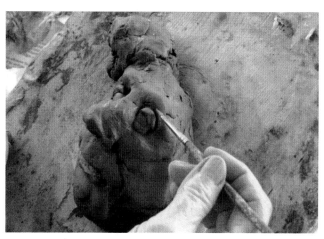

At this point I really haven't done much to the original lump of clay, but only a few more details are needed. First, of course, he needs some eyes. I just make two small balls and push them into the eye socket. Next, I add very simple upper and lower eyelids, and use a small damp brush to smooth the clay around the eye.

After ...

Then I use the handle of an old paint brush to push an indentation into his ear, and the sculpture is finished. The result is a cheerful fellow with a broken nose and a very strange haircut.

What did I learn?

I'm glad I left the weird blob that sort-of represents hair. I can't explain why I like it, but I do. It's a challenge to not 'fix' things that aren't realistic, but when I refrain myself I'm often happily surprised by the result.

THE CHEERFUL OGRE

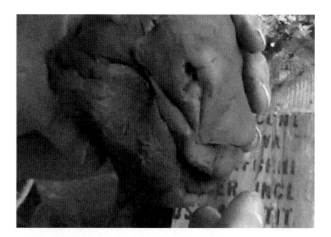

This is the second Fast Face I ever made. I didn't see any features at all on the lump of clay when I pulled it out of the bag. Fortunately, I had the video camera turned on while I made him so I could show this new method to my You-Tube subscribers.

When I started writing this book I went back to watch the video, and I was shocked to see several very nice features — and even two complete faces — in the original ball of clay. I even missed the two round eyeballs on the lump of clay that I used for the nose. You can see some of the features I missed here. (I grabbed the photos from the video, so they're a little fuzzy.)

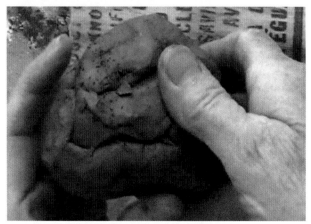

What does this tell me? I'm getting better at the mental trick Leonardo used to find meaningful images in random shapes and shadows.

Am I sad about not finding those other three faces? Not at all — I really like the face I ended up with, weird nose and all.

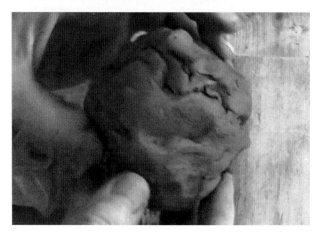

Before...

I didn't have anything to work with (or so I thought) so I squished the ball of clay and then folded it over. This gave me a strange but very well-defined mouth. Now it just needed the rest of the head to turn it into a face.

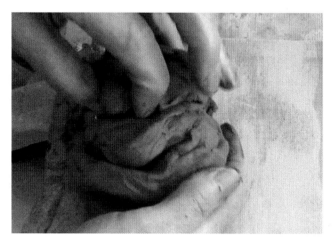

The nose started out as a rough lump of clay. I pressed my fingers into the new lump to make nostrils. I got a little carried away, especially since normal-looking nostrils were already suggested by the clay. Let's call it creative license.

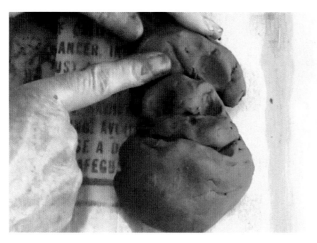

I pressed the clay onto my wooden stand and added more clay for his eyes and forehead. This is not a very bright ogre because he has very little room for a brain.

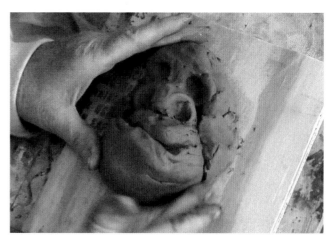

Deep eye sockets were pressed into the clay, and then another piece was added on each side for cheeks. I'm leaving everything quite rough.

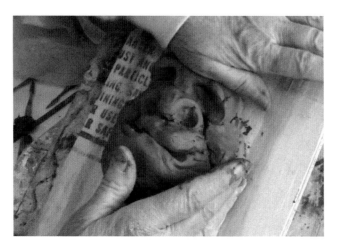

To make a heavy brow ridge I pressed down with the heal of my hand. I defined the lower lip with a fast swipe of my thumb, and added a dimple in the middle of his chin. Then I added eyes. I made two small balls of clay, pressed them in-

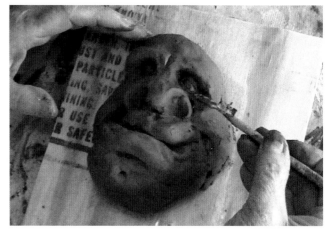

to the eye sockets, and then outlined the upper and lower lids with a wax carving tool.

After . . .

I gave him two small ears, and he was done. In spite of a nose that would embarrass even a Neanderthal, he seems quite pleased with himself.

(If you'd like to watch the video I made when I sculpted the Cheerful Ogre, you'll find a link to it on the Resource Page.)

What I learned.

You can get away with a lot of silliness without losing the 'face-ness' of a sculpt. It still reads as a face if there are two eyes, a bump that's sort of nose-like, and a mouth. In fact, you can leave out everything except the eyes and it still almost works.

Because of these practice sessions, I'm starting to loosen up and let the clay do more of the work. There's something very special that happens when a lump of clay seems to be looking back at you, even when the sculpt isn't perfect.

I'm sure our ancient ancestors got that feeling even more powerfully than we do, because they weren't bombarded by images and advertisements and videos all day long. Can you imagine what it would have been like to go into the caves at Lascaux by torch light, 20,000 years ago, and see those magnificent animals dancing in the firelight? Even the people who created the paintings would have seen their animals come to life.

That's magic.

HECTOR

This lump of clay looked like an almost complete hound dog. To see what I mean, turn the book counter-clockwise and look at the large photo on the right. It has a nice floppy ear and a pointy nose, a mouth and an eye. A Labrador retriever, perhaps — but I didn't want to make a dog.

What I learned.

The clay can help, but it's *not* in charge. I was in the mood for a whimsical and silly human face, and after some fairly rough handling, the clay obliged. (Although Hector does look like a fellow who would like to have a good hunting dog by his side.)

I started by pushing up on the ridge that could have defined a dog's ear and turned it into a smiling mouth, as shown below.

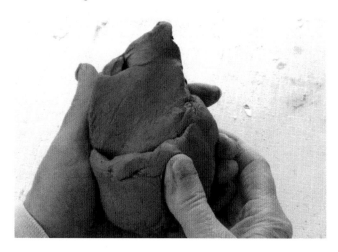

Before...

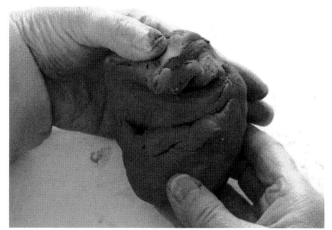

Now I had a mouth, but nothing else. I pushed down on the point at the top to see if I could get a nose-like appendage. It's close ...

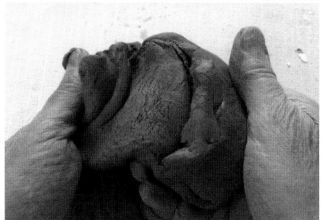

...but the upper lip was too flat. I bent the whole thing backwards and then forwards again to get a nicer curve to the upper lip. He's still got a pronounced underbite, but the mouth is now more believable.

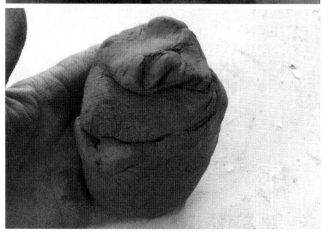

I squashed that pointy nose back, which left a few extra marks that don't quite belong there. However, it already has the suggestion of a nostril on one side.

I pulled a new lump of clay out of the bag and was about to flatten it for the upper half of the face. Then I looked at the new piece sitting on top of his head and it looked like hair to me. (Or was it a hat?) I decided to keep it. I removed the new piece temporarily and added eyes just above the nose. Then I put the hair back on. Yes, by this time I've firmly decided that it's hair, even though the name Carmen Miranda keeps popping into my head...

DOES YOUR INNER CRITIC DRIVE YOU NUTS?

Even when we're making something just for fun, we often have a voice in our mind that 'helps' us with suggestions, criticism, and judgments every time we make a creative decision. Then self-doubt creeps in, and the project isn't fun any more.

Writers have this problem, too. If they try to edit their work as they write, it removes the spontaneity that could make their work more lively and readable. That's because writing and editing require two different parts of the brain, and the two parts don't work well to-gether. The same thing is true for any form of creative expression, including sculpting.

Here's a trick (actually a form of meditation) that might help you silence your inner critic. Just tell the voice, respectfully, that you appreciate the help — but right now you need to be thinking about something else. It can be surprisingly effective if you practice it mindfully. Uninvited judgments will start to appear less often, your work will become more genuine, and you'll have more fun as you sculpt, paint or write. But what if ...

To finish Hector, I added small ears. I don't put ears on all of my Fast Faces, but this one seemed to need them. I pulled the long point on the side of the hair and gave it a little twist, but I didn't want to get too carried away. I really like the spontaneously whimsical nature of this fellow, and I didn't want to lose it.

I added a smile muscle to one corner of his mouth and smoothed off just the eyes with a very soft small watercolor brush. Then I finished him with a small bow tie below his oversized chin.

I left the cracks on his upper lip that formed when I bent the clay backwards (I think it looks like stubble) but I smoothed off the extra dip in his nose.

I made a lot of decisions when I made this fellow. Try going back over the photo series and imagine what you would have done differently. Maybe you would have made the dog, instead?

... **what if** the critic isn't your own self-doubt but a real person who likes to stand over your shoulder and give helpful suggestions while you work? They're trying to be supportive, but it's hard to create spontaneously when you have an audience.

Try explaining this to them in a respectful way. That might work. If it doesn't, find a more private place to play with your clay. You can let them see your work a few days later, when you don't feel so personally attached to it and their helpful suggestions and critiques won't bother you so much.

After ...

Before ...

ESMERELDA

This lump of clay didn't give me much to work with. In fact, I did a lot of squishing and folding before I even got this suggestion of a mouth. It's not much, but it was enough to get me started.

Almost all of the other faces in this book are male, with the exception of poor Great Aunt Agatha on page 62. I kept looking for feminine features, but they don't seem to show up very often in my lumps of clay. Those lips did have promise, though. Esmerelda didn't end up with the face of a fashion model, but I kind of like her.

What did I learn?

If the clay doesn't give you what you want, work with what you have and keep working until you like what you see. There is absolutely nothing left on the final sculpt that was on the original lump of clay, but sometimes just a suggested starting place is all you need.

I think the very vague suggestion of a small nose was what drew me to this lump of clay. So many of my other faces end up with humongous noses, and a smaller one would be a nice change.

I started by adding clay to give me space for eyes and a forehead, and I shaped the lips a little better. The new lump of clay had a suggestion for one eye, and almost an eyebrow. I'll be paying attention to them as I work.

First, though, I needed to start with a small nose. Then I gave her some cheeks and a nasolabial fold on both sides of the mouth. Small laugh muscles were added at the corners of her mouth, and I've started to change the mouth to make her smile.

I added small eyes and eyebrows, following the suggestions that I found in the clay. She got a pointy chin, and I added some clay to the nose to make it pointy, too.

I gave her a short perky hairdo and she was almost done, but I wasn't happy with the mouth. The corners of the lower lips were wider than the upper lips, which isn't realistic. OK, the rest of her isn't realistic, either, but I wanted a better smile.

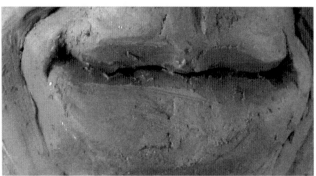

This is how her lips looked before I 'corrected' the shapes given to me by my lump of clay. You can see that the corner of the lower lip extends beyond the upper lip, which is not the way lips usually look.

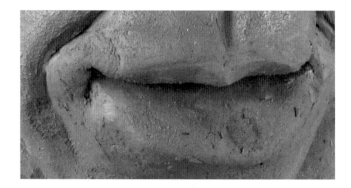

I carved away some of the lower lip at the corners of her mouth, and reduced some of the fullness of the lower lip. This gave her a more relaxed smile.

I also removed some of the extra clay at her jaw line that made her look fat. I wanted to emphasize that pointy chin because it gives a nice contrast to the full lips.

Those high eyebrows make me think she's questioning something, or she just received a pleasant surprise. Did Hector just propose? If he did, will she accept him?

CUDDLES MALOY

I couldn't decide if this face was supposed to be a man with a big mustache or a Shih tzu — and that was a real problem. If it hadn't been for that lower lip, I probably would have sculpted a dog with a short muzzle. But I *liked* that lower lip, and I wasn't willing to give it up.

What did I learn?

Long after this lump of clay was squished up and put back in the bag I thought of a simple 'fix,' but by then it was too late. I'll tell you what it was at the end of this chapter.

On the bright side, the best way to learn a new skill is to try things and see what happens. You can't expect a masterpiece every time you sit down to play with a ball of clay. In fact, every error is an important opportunity for improving your craft.

Take a look at the photo below and try to imagine what you'd do with it. When you get to the *after* picture, see if you think it has the same flaws I think it has. It's OK if you disagree with me. (A friend told me it's his favorite of all the Fast Faces in this book.)

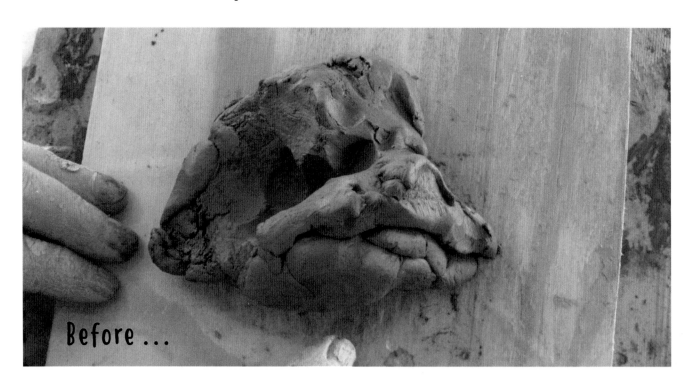

Before ...

On the original lump of clay I could definitely see a mouth and a nose. I cut off part of the clay to give me a nice flat area that could be put on the board, and I chose to cut it so the face would be seen at an angle.

At this point I could have added more clay directly above the nose to give the face a more human-shaped skull, but I stayed on the fence.

I added a people-nose above the mouth, which looks a lot like a dog nose when it's stuck on the front of the muzzle and the nostrils are facing forwards like this.

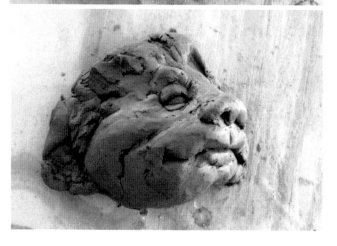

I tried to make up for it by connecting the nose to the forehead, but that left no brow ridge (what we'd call a 'stop' on a dog's head). Then I filled in the deep recess behind the muzzle to create a cheek, and added eyes and eyebrows.

I gave him a goatee to make up for his lack of a proper chin. Then I added just the hint of an ear. This face does have potential, perhaps as an overweight Victorian dandy, but I gave up on it and stuck the clay back in the bag.

What I learned.

I would have been happier with Cuddles Maloy if the eyes were higher and further apart. I put them where the clay 'told' me to, and in this case the clay made a mistake. He still wouldn't have the normal proportions and shape of a real human, but none of my other Fast Faces do either.

Here's a tip for you: I didn't see this simple fix until I looked at the photo below. If you ever have a sculpture that isn't quite working but you can't figure out what's wrong, take a photo.

Or look at the sculpture in a mirror. If you look at your work in a new way it might trick your brain into seeing details you didn't notice before.

After ...

ART IS MEDICINE FOR THE SOUL.

Since my blog went online back in 2008 I've been getting emails from people who say that my tutorials, books and videos about sculpting changed their lives. Those emails are the best possible reward for the work I do, but I'm sure all authors who teach art get the same kind of emails. It's the art itself that's special, not me.

Some of these folks tell me their new art projects have brought them out of chronic depression. Some people tell me they've been physically disabled for a long time. They're still disabled, of course, but now it doesn't bother them as much because they have something new to look forward to every day. People who have PTSD because of traumatic events in their lives now feel more engaged with the world, and they're better able to cope.

I think I now understand how art can have such a positive affect on someone's well-being. Mihaly Csikszentmihalyi, the author of *Flow: The Psychology of Optimal Experience*, believes a special kind of experience is important for both creativity and well-being, and these experiences are often "the best moments in our lives." When you're in this state he calls *flow*:

1. You're completely focused on the task.
2. You're clear about your goals, and you get immediate feedback to let you know if you've achieved them.
3. You lose track of time.
4. The project is intrinsically rewarding.
5. There's a comfortable balance between challenge and skills.
6. Actions and awareness are merged, so you temporarily lose your sense of self and your inner critic.

That sounds like an art project when it's going well, doesn't it? (And it's very similar to the way Temple Grandin described the power of curiosity in *Animals Make us Human*.) All kinds of art make us feel like that. Not just sculpting, but writing, painting, woodworking, gardening — even doodling and using Copic Markers in a coloring book. When we're totally focused on a project that contains many small problems that must be solved, we have an opportunity to experience flow. The experience of flow makes us feel good, and that makes us happy. It also relieves stress. That's one of the reasons why Dr. Csikszentmihalyi calls it an "optimal experience."

But according to author Martin Seligman, to truly *Flourish*, (the title of his latest book), we need to go beyond just occasionally feeling good and being happy. We also need engagement, meaning, accomplishment, and positive relationships in our lives. Art can help with these things, too:

- We become **more engaged** when we share our work — or even better, when we teach our craft to other people.
- Art helps us **find meaning** in the world around us, and helps us learn what matters most to us so we can stop 'sweating the small stuff.'
- We become **accomplished** as we push ourselves to improve our skills,
- And we **gain positive relationships** as we join communities that share our interests.

Isn't that just another way of saying that *art is medicine for the soul?*

SHORT & SWEET

Now I'll show you a few more of my Fast Faces, with just the *before* and *after* photos. As always, try to imagine what *you* would have done with these same lumps of clay if you had them in your hand.

Great Aunt Agatha

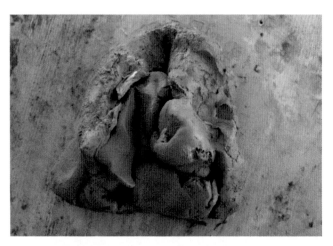

Once again, I got carried away with the size of the nose. The original lump of clay had a mouth pushed up under a large misshapen bump that suggested a nose, and the clay on one side looked like hair. The hair is the only thing I didn't change. However, all of the features were suggested, more or less, by the clay.

I do hope Agatha isn't too self-conscious about the huge honker I stuck on her face.

The Professor

I was really hoping the bee-stung lips on this lump of clay would let me create a woman — a woman who was younger than Great Aunt Agatha, and with a smaller nose. That obviously didn't happen. I played with the upper lip to make it slightly more feminine, but then I added another big nose and the bushy eyebrows, and 'she' clearly became a 'he.'

I don't think my clay has anything against young women, (or young men, for that matter), but it doesn't show me very many beautiful young faces of either sex. I think it's because I really enjoy sculpting people with a lot of character on their face, and you get that kind of face by living an interesting life.

Like most of the faces that I make using the Fast Face method, the features are not in the right place for a real human, but they still work.

Grumpy Gramps

I made many changes to this ball of clay, but the face I sculpted was based on the suggestions I found in the clay. Those 'suggestions' were not very well-defined, so I had a lot of options to play with. He definitely looked grumpy, though, right from the start. He reminds me of a neighbor I once had who was never happy unless he had something to be angry about.

I don't hang around with perpetually-scowling people very often (life is too short) so I did a Google Image search to help me get a fairly realistic growl on Gramp's face.

The squinty eyes were suggested by the clay. The clay also hinted that the nose should be very short. The one he ended up with is still short, but not as flat, and it's pointing in a different direction. The bald-on-top hairdo was on the clay to start with.

Even though Gramps is growling, I'm rather attached to him. I keep wondering what he's so mad about — and if I knew, would I be mad about it, too?

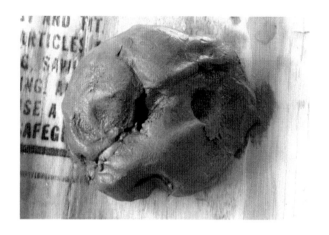

No Bath Charlie

I happened to be holding this lump of clay at the same time that I was looking at my dog Charlie (right after saying the "B" word). That's when I knew what to do with it.

I just added a few squiggles to indicate fur, two round balls for eyes, and a doggy nose. Done.

The original lump of clay looked scared, but the strong vertical line I added above one eye to help define the ear made him look angry. That was not my intention. It's always surprising when one small line or gesture makes such a big difference in the mood on a sculpted face.

The original shapes could have been made into a child, but I decided to let it be a dog — and then I stuck with that decision. That's something I *didn't* do when I made Cuddles Maloy, and I regretted it. Lesson learned, lesson applied.

Mr. Barnaby

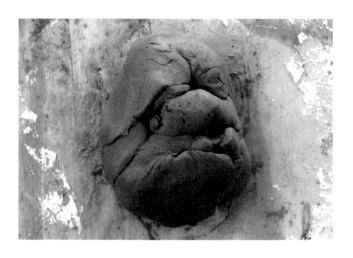

I made so few changes to this lump of clay that they're hard to find on the photo below. I didn't want to do anything that would change that expression, with those squinty hooded eyes and a mouth that folds up into puckers on one side.

I never would have designed a face like Mr. Barnaby if the clay hadn't done most of it for me.

I enjoy this particular face because it would take an entire life story to explain why he looks the way he does. Who *is* this fellow? What has he seen in life that makes him so sad? Is he lonely? Tired? The writer in me really wants to know.

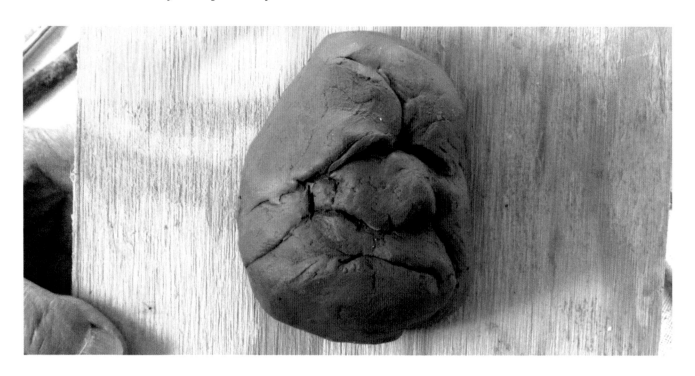

NOW IT'S YOUR TURN

You've now had a chance to watch over my shoulder as I made some fast faces, so grab some clay and start making some faces of your own. I hope you're pleasantly surprised by every single one you make.

30 day Fast Face challenge.

A personal challenge is fun and it's a great way to keep yourself motivated. Commit yourself to making at least one Fast Face every single day for at least 30 days. They only take a few minutes, so it's an easy commitment to keep. Take a photo of each one, and keep them in order.

Did you learn something when you made a face? Write it down, even if it sounds silly.

Did you like the way it came out? Don't be shy — go ahead and admit that it's a small masterpiece.

Are there things you wish you'd done differently? That means you've just learned something — and that's something we should always celebrate!

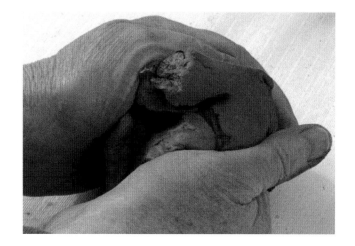

SHARE AND SAVE

The WED clay I recommend for Fast Faces can't be fired in a kiln, but you can still share them with your friends or save them for yourself. You can also use them for other projects. Here are a few ways to do that.

Use them as models for animated videos, a graphic novel or children's book.

Many of your Fast Faces will have unique personalities to go with their unusual proportions and features. As an author, I'm itching to write a story that explains the mood they're in, or create the imaginary world they might be living in. (They certainly aren't living in *this* world, after all.)

Make a quick sketch of one of your favorite faces from several different angles. Then sketch again, exaggerating one feature, perhaps, or changing the shape of the head. Keep at it until you have a character you can use for your next project.

Share on Instagram or Facebook.

This is easy. Just take snapshots of the Fast Faces you make and send them to your favorite image sharing site. Use a hashtag like #FastFaces, and be sure to include the title of this book so people who like your images can learn how to make Fast Faces of their own.

Share the Fast Face experience.

If your friends, grandparents, kids or grandchildren show an interest in learning how to make Fast Faces, why not invite them over for a party? Make sure you have enough clay on hand so everyone has enough for at least one face, and then let the giggling begin. You can also

check with your local senior center. They're usually looking for interesting things their members can do, and I know many retirees would love to have an excuse to play with some clay.

Put photos in a scrapbook.

Scrapbooking is fun, and Fast Faces are fun, so why not combine the two? Take photos of your faces and print them, or make drawings that will fit on the pages of a scrapbook. If you'd like to use your book as a journal, you can add notes about each one. Put the date and a few remarks about how you feel about the face, what you learned, and what you would do differently if you did it again.

Draw or paint portraits of your Fast Faces.

If you can't get your friends and family to hold still long enough to model for you, you can use your Fast Faces as models, instead, like these practice sketches by my daughter, Jessie Rasche. Your clay faces won't move while you draw, which is handy, and they don't get bored or talk while you're trying to draw them, either. The fact that they're all one color makes it easy to see how the shadows you draw on your paper create the illusion of rounded forms.

Your drawings can go into your journal or scrapbook. If you keep them in order, you'll be able to go back and see how much they've changed since you first started making them.

Let your faces dry, and paint them.

WED clay isn't waterproof when it dries, and areas that stick out, like ears and locks of hair, can be easily broken off. However, if the face was made from one piece of clay, there's a possibility that it will dry evenly without cracking. There's no guarantee, but it's worth a try. Just leave it uncovered for a few days until it's no longer cold to the touch.

It won't be a permanent sculpture, of course, because it will turn back into mud if it gets wet. However, my grandson made a little heart five years ago using WED clay, and it survived until just a few months ago when my cat knocked it off the shelf.

If you want to paint the face to see what it would look like with real people-colors, you can spray it with white primer when it's completely dry. Then add color with acrylic paints. If you don't have a clumsy cat, your unfired clay face might last for years. Take a photo, though, just in case. Then you'll have a permanent record, and you'll have another image to share on your Social Media accounts.

Make a plaster cast.

I left this idea to last because most of the other ideas are easier and they're much less expensive. To make a good plaster cast you'll need a flexible mold, and the best material I've found is Rebound 25 brushable silicone from the Smooth-On company. It comes in two containers marked A and B, and you mix equal parts together to make your mold. You'll also need a thickener for your second and third coats. A starter pack will cost about $40.00, and it will be enough for three or four fist-sized clay faces.

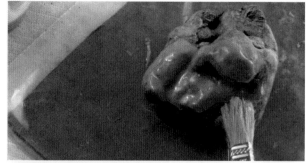

I won't give you all the details here, because it's really best to watch videos, either on the manufacturer's site or on YouTube. I'll put links to my favorite mold-making videos on the downloadable Resources list (page 72). However, some videos recommend expensive resin products for the 'mother mold,' the thin shell that holds the flexible silicone in the proper shapes while you're pouring your plaster. A few layers of plaster cloth works just fine and it's much less expensive.

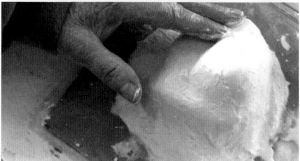

I'll add a few photos of the process here so you can see what's involved in making a silicone mold, but remember — the silicone product is *expensive*, so make sure you watch some experts doing it before trying it yourself.

First, let your Fast Face dry out enough so the brush won't distort the features. Spray your dried sculpture with a clear varnish (Krylon Crystal Clear works well, but any clear spray paint will work) and let it dry. You don't need a release.

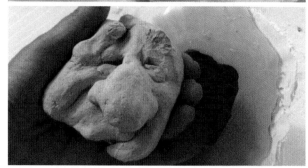

The two-part silicone needs to be carefully mixed in equal quantities. These faces are so small that small medicine cups work well for measuring. Then the material is brushed over the face in a very thin layer. There will be many undercuts and thin, narrow depressions in your Fast Face, and these areas will trap air that must be released because bubbles will show up on the final plaster casting.

You'll need several coats, and you'll need the thickener that's made for the silicone product for the second and third coats. There's a wait time between coats, so it will take several hours to finish a mold.

When the silicone cures you'll need a hard shell to hold your flexible silicone mold in the right shape while you're pouring your plaster. I use a few layers of plaster cloth.

In the photos on the previous page I'm pouring concrete instead of plaster, because I want to put my Fast Face outside in my flower garden. The process is just the same as pouring plaster, but concrete is waterproof. Plaster can't be left outside.

When the plaster is hard you can remove it from the mold. If all goes well, you'll have a perfect copy of your Fast Face. Let it dry for several days and then paint it with acrylic paints, or leave it white.

What's next?

Now that you've had fun making your Fast Faces, you may want to learn more about sculpting with clay. I'll put links to my favorite books and videos on the downloadable resources page.

If your local community center has a ceramics program with some kilns they'll let you use, ask them to show you how to finish your Fast Faces so they can be fired. You'd need to use regular pottery clay instead of the WED clay I used in this book, and you'll need to learn how to hollow out the back side of your sculptures to

Oscar, my very first Fast Face, was cast in plaster. You can see a larger photo of him on page 6. When the plaster was dry I sprayed him with white primer. Then I used a thin acrylic glaze of Burnt Umber that I quickly wiped off, leaving color in the dips and creases.

keep them from blowing up in the kiln. (That's not as scary as it sounds, but it is disappointing). They might also have some interesting classes in pottery or sculpture that will give you more experience working with clay.

You might also enjoy learning how to draw interesting characters, or maybe you'd like to draw or paint faces that look like real people. You'll find some of my favorite drawing and painting books on the resource page.

RESOURCES

For a downloadable list of places where you can find the materials and supplies you'll need for your Fast Faces, go to:

https://www.UltimatePaperMache.com/FastFaces

You'll also find links to some of my favorite YouTube videos and other resources that I think you'll find useful. I'll try to keep the resource page updated, but links do change. If you find a link that's broken, please let me know so I can fix it. You can contact me at **Jonni@jonnigood.com**.

If you send an email, be sure to put "Fast Faces" in the subject line so your email doesn't get accidentally deleted.

While you're at UltimatePaperMache.com for the resource page, be sure to stop in at the Daily Sculptors page, too, and say hi. There's a link to it at the top of the site. We have a great community of sculptors of all ages who visit that page often, and we'd love to hear from you.

I hope you'll check out my YouTube channel, too. You can find it at:

https://www.youtube.com/user/UltimatePaperMache

ABOUT THE AUTHOR

I'm the host of the popular sculpting website UltimatePaperMache.com, where I share my innovative sculpting methods and recipes with a world-wide audience. My goal is to make sculpting so easy that everyone can have fun doing it.

I'm also the author of four other popular books about sculpting and two cozy mystery novels that feature an eccentric small-town sculptor who lives a much more exciting life than I do. I live in a small town in Minnesota with my pets and a house full of animal sculptures.

If you enjoyed this book I hope you'll leave a review on amazon.com. It would mean a lot to me, and your fellow readers will appreciate it, too.

You can see my other books at: http://amzn.to/2ty9F8V

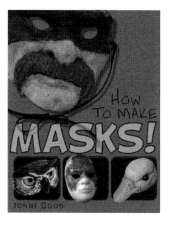

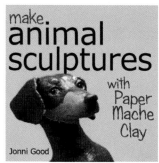

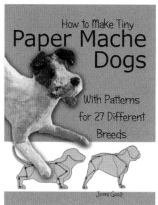

Made in the USA
Coppell, TX
20 May 2020

26189790R00045